MICHELANGELO
SCULPTOR, ARTIST AND ARCHITECT

ART HISTORY LESSONS FOR KIDS
Children's Art Books

Speedy Publishing LLC

40 E. Main St. #1156

Newark, DE 19711

www.speedypublishing.com

n this book, we're going to talk about the life of famous Renaissance artist Michelangelo. So, let's get right to it!

Sistine Chapel ceiling.

WHO WAS MICHELANGELO?

Michelangelo was one of the Italian Renaissance's most famous artists. He was a sculptor and a master with marble, but he was also a painter, a poet, and an architect.

Among his masterpieces are:

- The frescoes on the ceiling of the Sistine Chapel

- The monumental statue of the Biblical figure of David, and

- The Pietà, which is a statue of the Virgin Mary holding the crucified figure of Christ

Michelangelo Buonarroti.

EARLY LIFE

Born in 1475 near Tuscany in the city of Caprese, Italy, Michelangelo's full name was Michelangelo di Lodovico Buonarroti Simoni, but he eventually became so famous that he was known by just his first name. His father Lodovico had a position as a civil officer in the village. Michelangelo was the second boy in a family of five boys and he was still a baby when the family moved to Florence. His mother, Francesca Neri, was ill, so Michelangelo was nursed by a wet-nurse. A wet-nurse is a woman who breastfeeds another woman's child.

At that time, Michelangelo was living with a stonemason's family. He joked later that in his wet-nurse's milk he drank the stone-cutting tools that he used to do his art. By this he meant that there was so much stone dust where he was living and he was surrounded by the stonemasons' work, so he absorbed it, just like a baby drinks milk. Sadly, his mother Francesca died when he was only 6 years old.

As a young boy, Michelangelo wasn't really interested in his regular school studies. Instead, he watched the artists at the churches nearby and copied the drawings that he observed there. When he was in grammar school, he had a friend named Francesco Granacci who was 6 years older than he was. It's believed that Francesco introduced his young friend to the well-known artist Domenico Ghirlandaio from the city of Florence.

Michelangelo's father realized that his son had no interest in being a banker or civil servant as he had been, so he arranged for Michelangelo to work in Ghirlandaio's workshop as an apprentice. At the age of 13, Michelangelo began to practice with the technique of painting frescoes, which are paintings created on wet plaster.

Moses by Michelangelo.

THE INFLUENCE OF THE MEDICI FAMILY

Michelangelo had only been working for a period of a year to become a master of the arts when something amazing happened. His teacher Ghirlandaio recommended that he apprentice at the home of the powerful Medici Family. At the time, Lorenzo de' Medici was the ruler of Florence. The Medici's lavish gardens were filled with classical sculptures.

Michelangelo lived and studied at the palace from 1489 to 1492 AD. This was an amazing time period for the young artist. He was able to study with Bertoldo di Giovanni, a highly respected sculptor. In addition to this incredible exposure to master artists, he also met important Scholars, Poets, and Humanists. Humanists were influential thinkers who favored culture, the arts, and all things that lifted up human experience.

Tomb of Lorenzo II de Medici.

Just as another famous artist of his time, Leonardo da Vinci, Michelangelo was very interested in human anatomy and he wanted to study the muscles of the body more precisely. He requested special permission from the Catholic Church to use dead bodies so he could dissect them and make artistic, yet realistic, sketches of them.

The chemicals in the corpses had a bad effect on Michelangelo's health, but he continued to do the dissections because he wanted to fully understand anatomy so he could show the details in his sculptures.

All these blended influences helped Michelangelo to create a unique artistic style. He used his understanding of the human muscles to give his sculptures an incredibly lifelike realism. His statues looked real, and yet, they had a heavenly beauty, as if the bodies were seen through the eyes of a poet. Michelangelo was still a teenager when he completed the relief sculpture of entangled legs and arms called the *"Battle of the Centaurs."*

Michelangelo, Centauromachia, 1492 ca.

Also, in this time period he completed the beautiful relief sculpture called *"Madonna della Scala,"* which means the *"Madonna of the Stairs."* Both these works show the genius Michelangelo had for sculpting.

Michelangelo, Madonna Della Scala, 1490 ca.

Interiors and architectural details of Medici chapel designed by Michelangelo.

EARLY ARTISTIC SUCCESS AND INFLUENCES

When Michelangelo was seventeen years old his life changed. In 1492, his patron, Lorenzo the Magnificent died and there was a lot of political conflict in Florence. Michelangelo traveled to Bologna, Italy were he continued to do research and study. He was able to return to Florence three years later to work as a sculptor. The style of his art was modeled after the masterpieces of Ancient Rome and Greece.

During this time, Michelangelo created a sculpture called the *"Sleeping Cupid."* It's not known whether Michelangelo used techniques to age the sculpture or whether the art dealer who was selling it buried the sculpture to age it. In any case, the art dealer passed it off as an antique from ancient Rome.

The Last Judgement by Michelangelo.

IONAS

Cardinal Riario of the diocese of San Giorgio purchased the sculpture, but demanded his money returned when he realized it wasn't a genuine antique. However, Riario was now impressed with the young sculptor's work and he had a change of heart. He let Michelangelo keep the money. He invited Michelangelo to Rome and Michelangelo traveled there and began the next chapter of his life.

Madonna and Child by Michelangelo, 1504.

The Capitoline Hill.

MICHELANGELO'S PERSONALITY

Michelangelo was very hard on himself and sometimes treated others with arrogance, which simply means he acted as if he was superior to them. To him, art came from an internal inspiration. He felt that the art was in the stone already and that his job as a sculptor was to free the art from being imprisoned in the stone.

The figures in his sculptures are powerful and dynamic even when they are seated. He tended to live as if he were poor no matter how much money he had, and frequently slept with his clothes and boots on. Today he would be described as a "loner," which simply means he preferred to be by himself working on his art.

Interiors of St. Peters Basilica - famous religious landmark.
Beautiful decoration with golden altar.

TWO OF MICHELANGELO'S MASTERPIECES

Michelangelo's arrival in Rome was another turning point for him. A second cardinal by the name of Jean Bilhères de Lagraulas showed an interest in his work. He commissioned Michelangelo to do a sculpture for his tomb. The Pietà, which means "compassion," was possibly Michelangelo's most ambitious work to date. It was carved from one piece of beautiful Carrara marble and was 6 feet wide and almost that tall.

The realism of the anatomy, the flowing fabric that looks like cloth although it is marble, and the emotion on the Virgin Mary's face as she grieves her dead son are all factors that make the Pietà a masterpiece. Michelangelo was only 25 years old when he completed it.

The Pieta is a statue by Michelangelo.

There's a legend that he overheard people talking and saying that his work was done by another sculptor. He boldly carved his name on Mary's sash. It's the only one of his works that he signed. The statue has been moved at least six times and it now resides in Vatican City at St. Peter's Basilica where thousands of visitors see it each year.

Visiting the the Basillica San Pietro. Pieta by Michelangelo.

When Michelangelo traveled back to Florence, he took on an even more challenging project. He was commissioned to create a sculpture of the Biblical hero of David. The sculpture was to be carved out of a single piece of marble that was 17 feet in height.

Two other sculptors had given up on the project because there were imperfections in the massive marble, but Michelangelo found a way to free the huge figure of David from the stone.

This masterpiece showing a young courageous man ready to take on a giant stands today in the Accademia Gallery in Florence and has become a symbol of the city. It was completed in 1504 when Michelangelo was 29 years old.

Michelangelo's David.

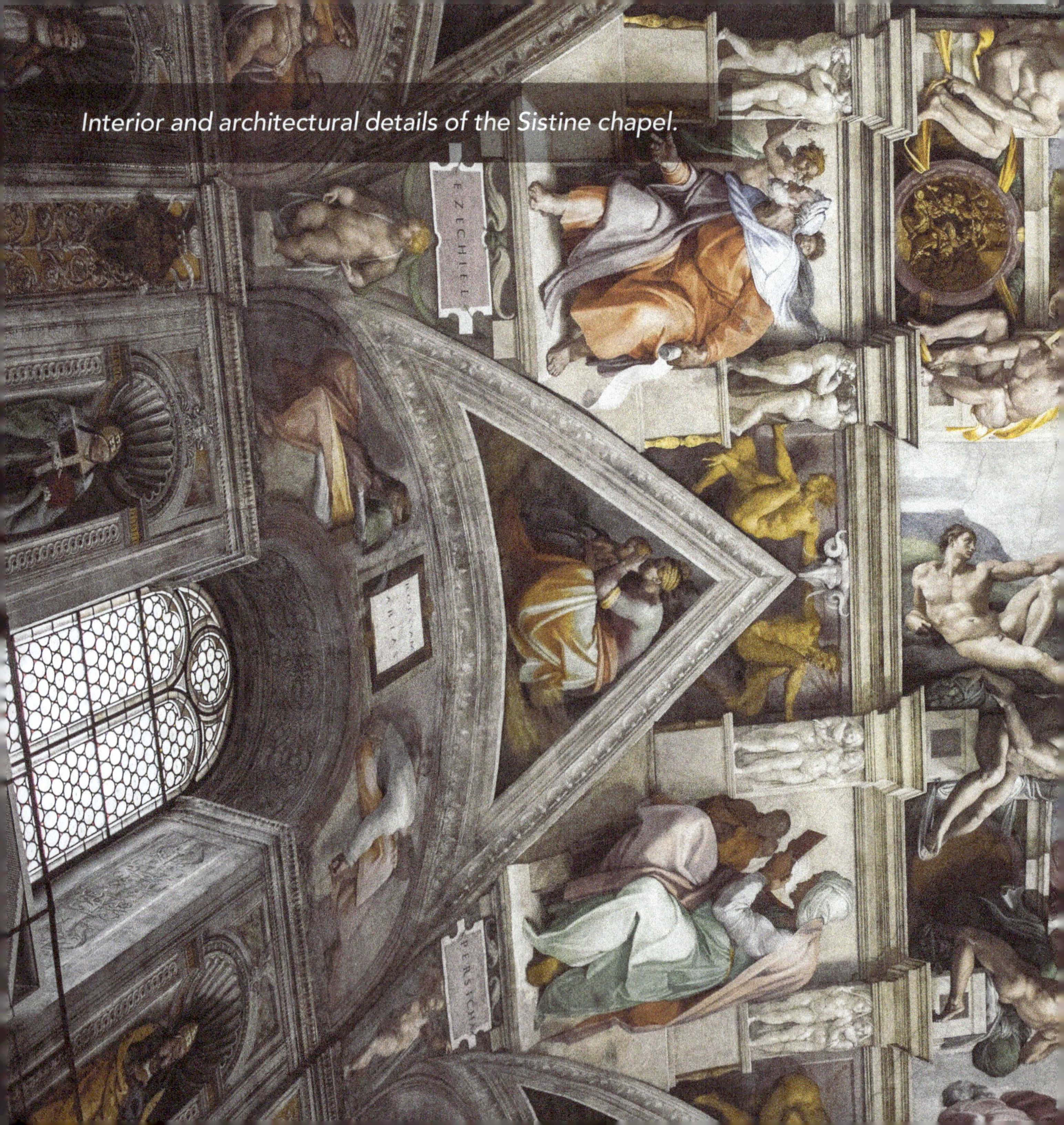

Interior and architectural details of the Sistine chapel.

DANIEL
CVMAEA

THE SISTINE CHAPEL

Pope Julius II commissioned Michelangelo to pause on his preparation of some statues for his tomb and design frescoes to adorn the ceiling of the Catholic Church's important Sistine Chapel. At the beginning, the painting was supposed to be the twelve apostles, but instead Michelangelo designed a series of stories from the Old Testament.

One of the most famous of these paintings is when God reaches out to touch the finger of Adam to give him life. Painting the ceiling while on scaffolding up near the top was very difficult and this project took its toll on the master artist's physical health. Despite the fact that Michelangelo didn't consider himself to be a painter, he painted one of the most famous masterpieces of all time.

For a while Michelangelo turned his attention to designing architectural wonders, such as the Medici Chapel as well as the Laurentian Library to house the enormous collection of books from the Medici family. The crowning glory of his architectural achievement was in 1546 when he was asked to be the chief architect in charge of the design of St. Peter's Basilica.

Michelangelo's redesign of the ancient Capitoline Hill included a complex spiralling pavement with a star at its centre.

A true Renaissance man, Michelangelo died at the age of 88 after a full life of impressive artistic achievements. His work continues to inspire artists in fields of sculpture, painting, and architecture today.

Awesome! Now you know more about the life and masterpieces of Michelangelo. You can find more Art books from Baby Professor by searching the website of your favorite book retailer.

Visit

BABY PROFESSOR
EDUCATION KIDS

www.BabyProfessorBooks.com
to download Free Baby Professor eBooks
and view our catalog of new and exciting
Children's Books